NORTH WAL

Dominated by impressive mountain ranges, steeped in history and bordered by splendid resorts with sandy beaches and bustling harbours, North Wales is full of variety and interest. The Snowdonia National Park covers 845 square miles of mountain, moorland and forest and of Snowdon's five peaks the loftiest, Y Wyddfa, is the highest mountain in Wales at 3,560 feet. Nowhere is the visitor far from the remains of an impressive castle. Edward I's great fortresses at Conwy, Caernarfon, Beaumaris and Harlech, are permanent reminders of the strategic importance of the area. Popular resorts and dignified Victorian towns line the coast, attracting many visitors, while the narrow-guage railways, many of them developed in the 19th century to serve the slate mining industry, have become tourist attractions in their own right.

Snowdon Mountain Railway

Llyn Crafnant

Snowdon from the Glyders

The **Snowdonia National Park** covers 845 square miles comprising mountain, moorland and forest, interspersed with deep valleys, and extends to the coast at Cardigan Bay. Among the mountain ranges are the Carnedds, Cader Idris, the Glyders and the Snowdon range. Of Snowdon's five peaks, the loftiest is Y Wyddfa which rises to 3,560 feet – the highest mountain in Wales. By far the easiest way to ascend Snowdon is by the picturesque Snowdon Mountain Railway, the only rack railway in Britain. The track climbs from the lakeside terminus at Llanberis to a point about 70 feet below the summit. Llanberis Pass, a deep cleft in the mountains where the River Seiont dashes down beside the road, provides some of the most spectacular views in all Wales. At the foot of the pass are Llyn Peris and Llyn Padarn, separated by a neck of land and guarded by Dolbadarn Castle, once a stronghold of the 13th century princes of Gwynedd.

Dolbadarn Castle

Llanberis Pass

Capel Curig lies 600 feet above sea-level amid wild and rugged mountain scenery. It is one of the oldest tourist centres in North Wales and is a fine base for walking and climbing. South of the village Moel Siabod rises to a height of 2,860 feet while the peaks of Snowdon stand out clearly to the west. They are particularly striking seen across the waters of Llyn Mymbyr which is also known as the Capel Curig lakes and consists of two small lakes linked by a channel.

Snowdon from Capel Curig

Tryfan and Cwm Idwal

The magnificent triangular peak of **Tryfan** rises to 3,010 feet above the valley of the River Llugwy. Its rock-strewn slopes are a challenge even to experienced climbers. Nearby Cwm Idwal is protected as a nature reserve and here the rare Snowdon lily grows.

At the head of the Nant Ffrancon Pass nearly 1,000 feet above sea-level lies picturesque **Llyn Ogwen**. This shallow lake, cradled between the Carnedd and Glyder mountains, is famous for its eels and trout. The Ogwen River rushes from it in a series of cascades best seen from the bridge which crosses the stream.

Betws-y-Coed

The Swallow Falls

One of the loveliest beauty spots of North Wales is the **Swallow Falls** which is situated on the River Llugwy some two miles west of Betws-y-Coed. Here the river rushes down from the nearby mountains through rocky chasms, hung with trees, on its way to join the Conwy River. Jagged rocks and crags divide the stream into a number of foaming cascades which tumble headlong over boulders between richly wooded banks.

Llyn Gwynant

Nant Gwynant is one of Snowdonia's finest valleys with splendid views of Snowdon. It lies between Beddgelert and Penygwryd and within it are two lakes. Llyn Dinas is named after the lakeside iron-age hill fort of Dinas Emrys, and Llyn Gwynant can justly claim to be one of the most beautiful lakes in Wales.

Llyn Dinas

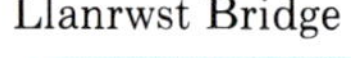

Llanrwst Bridge

The pleasant market town of **Llanrwst** is set amongst lovely scenery on the banks of the Conwy River. Here the Conwy Valley runs between lofty hills, wooded slopes and meadowland to the coast. Llanrwst is perhaps best known for the graceful stone bridge across the river. Built in 1636, the central arch rises to 60 feet. At the western end of the bridge stands Tu Hwnt I'r Bont, a 15th century cottage once used as a courthouse and now preserved by the National Trust.

Waterloo Bridge and River Conwy

The Fairy Glen

Betws-y-Coed

Ty Hyll, The Ugly House

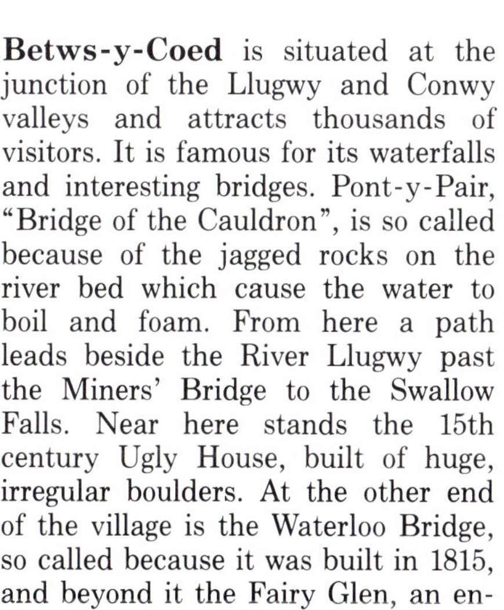

Betws-y-Coed is situated at the junction of the Llugwy and Conwy valleys and attracts thousands of visitors. It is famous for its waterfalls and interesting bridges. Pont-y-Pair, "Bridge of the Cauldron", is so called because of the jagged rocks on the river bed which cause the water to boil and foam. From here a path leads beside the River Llugwy past the Miners' Bridge to the Swallow Falls. Near here stands the 15th century Ugly House, built of huge, irregular boulders. At the other end of the village is the Waterloo Bridge, so called because it was built in 1815, and beyond it the Fairy Glen, an enchanting chasm with rocks and pools overhung by trees.

Aberglaslyn Pass

Beddgelert is a delightful village nestling at the foot of the mountains close to the junction of the Glaslyn and Colwyn Rivers. It is associated for all time with the story of Prince Llewelyn and Gelert, his faithful hound, whose grave gives the place its name. Beddgelert is a fine centre for walks and drives and a popular starting point among climbers for the ascent of Snowdon. Southwards runs the beautiful Pass of Aberglaslyn and on the northern side of the shallow Glaslyn estuary lies the little holiday village of Borth-y-Gest. **Porthmadog** stands on an inlet of Tremadoc Bay on land which was reclaimed from the sea in the early part of the 19th century. The town was once a flourishing port, its prosperity built on the slate trade. It is now a popular holiday centre with a busy harbour and fine views across the bay to the mountains of Snowdonia. Nearby the magnificent sweep of Black Rock Sands on the edge of the Glaslyn estuary is popular with summer visitors.

The Bridge, Beddgelert

Black Rock Sands

The Point, Borth-y-Gest

The Harbour, Porthmadog

The Dduallt Spiral, Festiniog Railway

Situated in the steep and beautifully wooded Vale of Ffestiniog, the village of **Ffestiniog** is a popular centre for mountain walking. **Blaenau Ffestiniog**, about three miles to the north, was an important centre for slate-quarrying. The blueish slate was used extensively for roofing, walling and paving but with the decline of the industry some of the underground galleries have now been opened up to tourists. The Festiniog Railway, oldest of the Welsh narrow gauge railways, was completed in 1836 to bring slate from the quarries of Blaenau Ffestiniog to Porthmadog for shipment. The railway closed in 1964 but has since been restored and is now a popular attraction with holidaymakers. Pleasantly situated on a wooded peninsula overlooking Traeth Bay near Porthmadog is the picturesque village of **Portmeirion**. It was created by the Welsh architect Clough Williams-Ellis in 1926 in the Italian style. With its campanile, castle and grottoes, Portmeirion attracts many visitors.

Portmeirion

Harlech Castle

Harlech Castle and the Morfa

Famous for its hill-top castle, the ancient town of **Harlech** is situated behind Tremadoc Bay. Built between 1283 and 1290 by Edward I, this magnificent fortress is strategically situated on a steep spur of rock overlooking the sea. Harlech Castle played an important part in the Wars of the Roses when it was a stronghold of the Lancastrians. The final seige, which was resisted staunchly and heroically but which ended in surrender, is commemorated in the song "Men of Harlech".

Dolgellau, situated in a fertile river valley beneath the slopes of Cader Idris, is an attractive market town. In the 18th century, the flannel trade was an important source of Dolgellau's prosperity and weaving was a flourishing cottage industry. Gold has been mined in the surrounding mountainsides since Roman times. Dolgellau gold was used for the Queen's wedding ring. **Cader Idris**, or Arthur's Seat, consists of a long mountain ridge of ancient volcanic rock rising to its summit, Pen-y-Cader, which is 2,927 feet high.

Cader Idris

Snowdonia from the Precipice Walk

Dolgellau is a centre for many fine walks of which **Precipice Walk** is probably the best known. Providing a circular walk of about seven miles, this starts near Llanfachreth and climbs to 800 feet affording splendid views of the lovely Mawddach estuary.

About two miles east of Dolgellau, the **Torrent Walk** traverses a delightful tree-shaded glen following the course of the little River Clywedog. This area provides numerous beautiful walks and here the Clywedog forms the torrent from which the walk is named.

The Fairbourne Railway

The little resort of Fairbourne lies on the south bank of the Mawddach estuary. From here the **Fairbourne Railway**, smallest of the Welsh narrow-gauge railways, runs through sand-dunes to Penrhyn Point where it connects with the ferry to Barmouth. Originally a horse-drawn tramway carrying building materials, it was converted for steam locomotives in 1916.

The Quay, Barmouth

The Estuary, Barmouth

Firm sands and a tiny harbour add to the quiet charm of the resort of **Barmouth**. Situated at the mouth of the Mawddach river, the town has a sandy beach to the north which provides excellent bathing. This is fine walking country. The Panorama Walk offers magnificent views of the town and of the estuary, surrounded by mountains. The mile long Barmouth Bridge carries the railway across the estuary and acts as a pedestrian promenade, giving magnificent views of Cader Idris.

The Gatehouse, Criccieth Castle

The **Lleyn Peninsula** is an unspoiled area of outstanding natural beauty with a number of pleasant resorts like **Criccieth**. This delightful little seaside town has a sand and rock beach facing Cardigan Bay and on an outcrop of rock stands the castle, fortified by Edward I. Westwards from Criccieth, the busy market town and resort of **Pwllheli** stands around a land-locked harbour. From Gimlet Rock, at the harbour mouth, the sands sweep five miles to the rocky, wooded headland of **Llanbedrog** with its sheltered, sandy cove. Around the headland, the unspoilt village of **Abersoch** has a small harbour in the mouth of the little Abersoch river. After Porth Neigwl, a sandy bay four miles wide, the Lleyn begins to narrow sharply and near the tip of the peninsular is **Aberdaron**, amid wild and rugged coastal scenery. On the Lleyn's north shore the twin fishing hamlets of **Morfa Nefyn** and **Porth Dinllaen** are dominated by the peaks of The Rivals which rise to 1,850 feet.

The Beach and Headland, Llanbedrog

The Harbour, Pwllheli

The Sands, Abersoch

The Beach, Aberdaron

The Rivals from Morfa Nefyn

Caernarfon Castle and Harbour

Caernarfon stands at the mouth of the River Seiont at the south-western end of the Menai Strait. As the ancient British fortress of Caer Seiont, the Roman military station of Segontium and, from 1284 to 1586, the administrative centre of North Wales, the town has great historical associations. The superb castle, begun in 1283, is the largest of the great Edwardian Welsh defences. The walls enclose an area of about three acres and are up to nine feet thick in places with towers which reach to a height of 124 feet.

It was at Caernarfon that Edward I proclaimed his eldest son Prince of Wales in 1301. This title has passed by tradition to the eldest son of each monarch since that time and in 1969 Prince Charles was created Prince of Wales here also.

From the towers of Caernarfon Castle it is possible to look landwards to the maze of narrow streets which comprise the old town. On the seaward side, the castle rises dramatically from the busy harbour where the quay offers boat trips as well as excellent fishing.

Upper and Lower Wards, Caernarfon Castle

Mary's Church by the white hazel pool, near the fierce whirlpool, with the Church of Tysilio by the red cave

The Menai Suspension Bridge

The **Menai Strait** separates Anglesey from the mainland. Telford's graceful suspension bridge which carries the Holyhead road 100 feet above the water was opened in 1826. The railway line for Holyhead crosses by Stephenson's Britannia Bridge, originally built in 1850 but largely rebuilt after a fire in 1970. Nearby is the village with the famous long name, a 58-letter tongue twister usually shortened to Llanfair P.G. It was here in 1915 that the first branch of the Women's Institute was formed. The university city of **Bangor**, on the south coast of the Menai Strait, is one of the most ancient cities of Wales. It owes its origins to the founding of a cathedral there in AD 548.

Bangor Pier

Penmon Priory

Puffin Island

Sixth century **Penmon Priory** is connected with the Celtic saint Seiriol who also established a monastic settlement on **Puffin Island**. Lying off the eastern tip of Anglesey, this island is now famous for the colonies of puffins which breed there.

The scenery of the **Isle of Anglesey** is mostly meadow and farmland with low-lying hills; very different from the mountainous mainland across the Menai Strait. At one time the island was important for the production of copper and lead ore but in recent times farming and fishing have become the main occupations of the inhabitants. The Anglesey Column was erected in 1816 in memory of the first Marquis of Anglesey. It stands 250 feet above sea-level and from the top of the column there are magnificent views.

The Anglesey Column

The Gateway, Beaumaris Castle

Beaumaris

Beaumaris is the principal town on Anglesey and, although small, it has some interesting corners. The superb moated castle was built by Edward I in 1295. With its imposing gatehouse and great round towers it is one of the best-known features on the island. It is also one of the finest examples of concentric fortification in Britain. This elegant little town has a sand and shingle beach and a fine pier which opened in 1846 and was for many years a port of call for pleasure steamers from Liverpool.

Port Amlwch

Amlwch is a bustling small town and port which was once the centre of a thriving copper industry. Nearby is **Bull Bay**. Formerly a busy ship-building port, this little resort has an attractive beach with rock pools and caves to explore. The rugged coastline of Anglesey abounds with quiet little seaside villages like **Cemaes**. Situated in a rock-girt bay, it has two sandy beaches and another of shingle. The tiny harbour is sheltered by a stone quarry and there are pleasant cliff walks.

Benllech is a popular seaside resort situated on the north coast of Anglesey. Set in a crescent-shaped bay, with fossil-studded cliffs, it has a fine beach of golden sand and is exceptionally safe for bathing and paddling.

Moelfre is a picturesque old fishing village built around a tiny cove on a rocky stretch of coastline which has been responsible for many shipwrecks. This area is rich in prehistoric monuments, notably the Lligwy Burial Chamber and the village of Din Lligwy.

Benllech Bay

Cemaes Bay

Trearddur Bay

The Sands, Rhosneigr

Holy Island, just eight miles by barely four, is connected to the west coast of Anglesey by a causeway which carries the railway and the main road to Holyhead. Four Mile Bridge is the only other remaining crossing. Holyhead is the main sea link with Ireland. **Trearddur Bay**, with its long sandy beach, is popular with surfers and sailing enthusiasts while the clear waters of the bay also attract skin-divers. A small suspension bridge joins the tiny island of South Stack to the larger Holy Island. This is crowned by a 90 feet high lighthouse warning shipping of the dangers of this coast. Once the haunt of a notorious gang of wreckers, **Rhosneigr's** sandy beaches now see nothing more sinister than fishing boats, dinghies and surfers.

South Stack Lighthouse

Penmaenmawr from the Green Gorge

The Sychnant Pass

The Aber Falls

The Quay and Castle, Conwy

On the lively quay at Conwy stands a house claimed to be the Smallest House in Britain. It consists of just two rooms and measures 6 feet across by 10 feet 2 inches to the eaves.

The Smallest House

Conwy Castle

From Bangor the coast road passes through the village of **Aber**, with the dramatic Aber Falls close by, and then the quiet little resorts of **Llanfairfechan** and **Penmaenmawr**. From here the old road strikes inland over the picturesque Sychnant Pass. **Conwy** is one of the best examples of a medieval walled town in Britain. The massive walls with three double gateways and 21 towers are well preserved as also is the great castle begun by Edward I in 1283. Conwy was strategically sited to guard the wide estuary, now crossed by three graceful bridges.

The Pier and Little Orme, Llandudno

Rhos-on-Sea

The Marine Drive, Llandudno

Colwyn Bay together with neighbouring **Rhos-on-Sea** provides three miles of sandy beach with Colwyn Bay pier reaching seawards from the centre. The town is known for its safe bathing and is also popular for all kinds of watersports. Eirias Park, one of several attractive parks, overlooks the bay and a miniature railway runs along the promenade. The attractive little resort of Rhos-on-Sea is pleasantly situated at the western end of the bay. There is a small harbour and overlooking the sea is the rebuilt Chapel of St. Trillo, measuring only 12 feet by 6 feet; it is the smallest chapel in Wales. From Rhos there are splendid coastal views up to Rhyl and the estuary of the River Dee.

Colwyn Bay

One of the principal holiday resorts of Wales, **Llandudno** is grandly situated between two beaches and often called the "Queen of Welsh resorts". The two-mile sweep of sand and shingle known as the North Shore stretches between the imposing headlands of the Great Orme and the Little Orme. Here the splendid promenade curves round the bay and there is a fine pier, constructed in 1876, and attractive gardens. The West Shore, a vast expanse of sand at low-tide, overlooks Conwy Bay. The town, with its wide streets, was largely laid out in the mid-19th century before which Llandudno was only a cluster of miners' and fishermen's cottages. The Great Orme is pitted with caves and old copper mines where evidence has been found of occupation by Stone Age dwellers as well as Romans; the five mile long Marine Drive encompasses the headland. The Great Orme Tramway and a cable railway run to the summit complex and there are wonderful views, especially at sunset.

Great Orme Tramway, Llandudno

Mostyn Street, Llandudno

The Laburnum Arch, Bodnant

Bodnant Garden is the finest garden in Wales, famous for its magnificent collection of rhododendrons, camellias, magnolias and azaleas. It also has a remarkable laburnum archway and a number of attractive terraces. Laid out in 1875, the gardens extend over 80 acres with fine views across the Conwy valley to the Snowdon range.

Gwrych Castle, Abergele

Abergele is a small market town between Colwyn Bay and Rhyl, situated about one mile inland on the old coast road. It has an interesting 16th century church and just outside the town is Gwrych Castle. Despite its castellated, Norman appearance, it was built in 1814. The 202 feet high intricate spire of **Bodelwyddan's** Church is a well-known landmark. The church is known locally as "the marble church" because fourteen different varieties of marble were used in the interior.

Bodelwyddan Church

Rhyl, with its three miles of sands and many seaside attractions, is a noted centre for family holidays. The harbour is the oldest part of the sea front and provides safe moorings for yachts and fishing boats at the mouth of the River Clwyd. The promenade runs as far as Prestatyn, providing five miles of coastal walks. **Prestatyn** itself has a number of sandy beaches noted for their safe bathing. The 8th century Offa's Dyke ended here and some remains can be seen near the town.

The Harbour, Rhyl

Rhuddlan Castle

Situated strategically at the head of the fertile Vale of Clwyd, **Rhuddlan** was one of the massive medieval castles built in North Wales by Edward I. Moated on three sides, the fourth side is protected by the River Clwyd.

Inland from Rhyl, **Dyserth** is situated at the northern end of the Clydian Range. The village is well known for its waterfall which drops 40 feet into a gorge in the limestone hills. It was described by Dr. Johnson in 1774 as "a very striking cataract".

Bala Lake

Bala Lake Railway

The Horseshoe Pass, Llangollen